D1392443

THE ALNWICK GARDEN

the most imaginative modern
public garden ever created
anywhere in the world
for

everyone

and especially
for children

Our friendly and knowledgeable Garden team are only too willing to answer any questions you may have – please do not hesitate to ask.

contents

My vision for The Alnwick Garden by The Duchess of Northumberland 4

still to come 6

design team 8

a message from HRH The Prince of Wales 9

the story of The Alnwick Garden is a remarkable one 10

vision to reality 14

ten steps to heaven 16

the grand cascade 18

the ornamental garden 24

the rose garden 28

the woodland walk 32

throughout the year at The Alnwick Garden 34

friends of The Garden 36

education, training and learning at The Alnwick Garden 36

My vision for The Alnwick Garden
by The Duchess of Northumberland

A very warm welcome to The Alnwick Garden. Since we first opened the gates to the public, we have welcomed 300,000 visitors in our first year, which was way beyond our initial projections, and early signs indicate another successful year is already underway.

I am delighted and impressed by the quality and standard of what has been created so far, as I hope you will be, and, as we continue to develop, I can promise you that we will never compromise on that quality. However, for me, this is just the beginning.

My vision is to create a beautiful public space accessible to everyone: a place of contemplation; a place of fun; a place of inspiration and education.

My task is to continue to raise funds to complete the vision: a pavilion, water, lighting, a poison garden, a serpent garden, a grass labyrinth, and a garden for the senses - all open into the night. My hope is to create a spectacular venue, a theatre of water, light and music, which will leave you, the visitor, spellbound, mesmerised and eager to return.

I very much hope you enjoy your visit to The Alnwick Garden, whether as a newcomer, or as a regular visitor, and that you too will visit again - soon.

Jane Northumberland

An artist's aerial view of The Garden proposals, showing the myriad of water courses, features, hedges, plantations and buildings.

still to come

The Grand Cascade, Rose and Ornamental Gardens have all been completed.

Still to come are stunning new gardens, with smaller, more specialised intimate spaces. There will be a **Garden for the Senses**, where texture, smell and sound take precedence. Other areas include a **Poison Garden**, a throwback to the Middle Ages, but also a practical and entertaining part of our education programme. In every garden, water will play a key role in helping to bring each area to life.

1 The Serpent Garden

2 The Spiral Garden feature

3 The Grass Labyrinth in Autumn

4 The Spiral Garden

5 The Poison Garden

6 The Garden for the Senses

5

6

design team

The Duchess selected the world-renowned Belgian landscape designer Jacques Wirtz and his son Peter to create The Garden. Sir Michael Hopkins, recognised as one of the leading international architects, has been appointed to prepare an overall masterplan and to design the new visitor facilities at The Garden.

Jacques Wirtz

Born 1924, Antwerp, Belgium.
Studied Landscape Architecture and Horticulture at the Tuinbouwschool Vilvoorde. Founder of *Wirtz Landscape Architecture* and *Wirtz International*, contracting and design companies. Designer of gardens and parks throughout Europe and Worldwide.

Peter Wirtz

Born 1963, Schoten.
Studied Landscape Architecture at the Tuinbouwschool, Melle. Since 1986 worked as a Landscape Architect for *Wirtz International* and *Wirtz Landscape Architecture*.

Sir Michael Hopkins

Sir Michael Hopkins is a Senior Partner of Michael Hopkins and Partners, which he founded in 1976. He has been awarded a CBE and knighted for Services to Architecture, and won the RIBA Gold Medal for Architecture in 1994.

ST. JAMES'S PALACE

Alnwick Castle and its great park lie at the heart of some of Britain's finest scenery, and the huge castle garden forms an integral part of the landscape.

Created over three generations from the middle of the 18th century, the garden in its prime reflected the personal commitment and vision of successive Dukes of Northumberland and the professional skill of gardeners of the highest reputation, such as Lancelot Brown, Decimus Burton, and W.A. Nesfield. This was to become one of Britain's most admired gardens, enjoying a century of magnificence and splendour which was brought to an end by war and severe financial restraint some fifty years ago.

In seeking to recapture the lost world of this great garden, and sharing it with others, the present Duchess of Northumberland is taking up once more the innovative ideas so brilliantly demonstrated in previous generations. The proposed designs will not simply recreate the past, but also provide for a variety of educational and botanical uses needed in the century to come.

The project is a bold and ambitious one which I am delighted to support. The restored garden will be a true work of art for everyone to enjoy, and a statement both of gratitude to the past and hope for the future. I wish the project every possible success.

Charles

HRH Prince Charles and the Duchess of Northumberland at the opening of The Alnwick Garden.

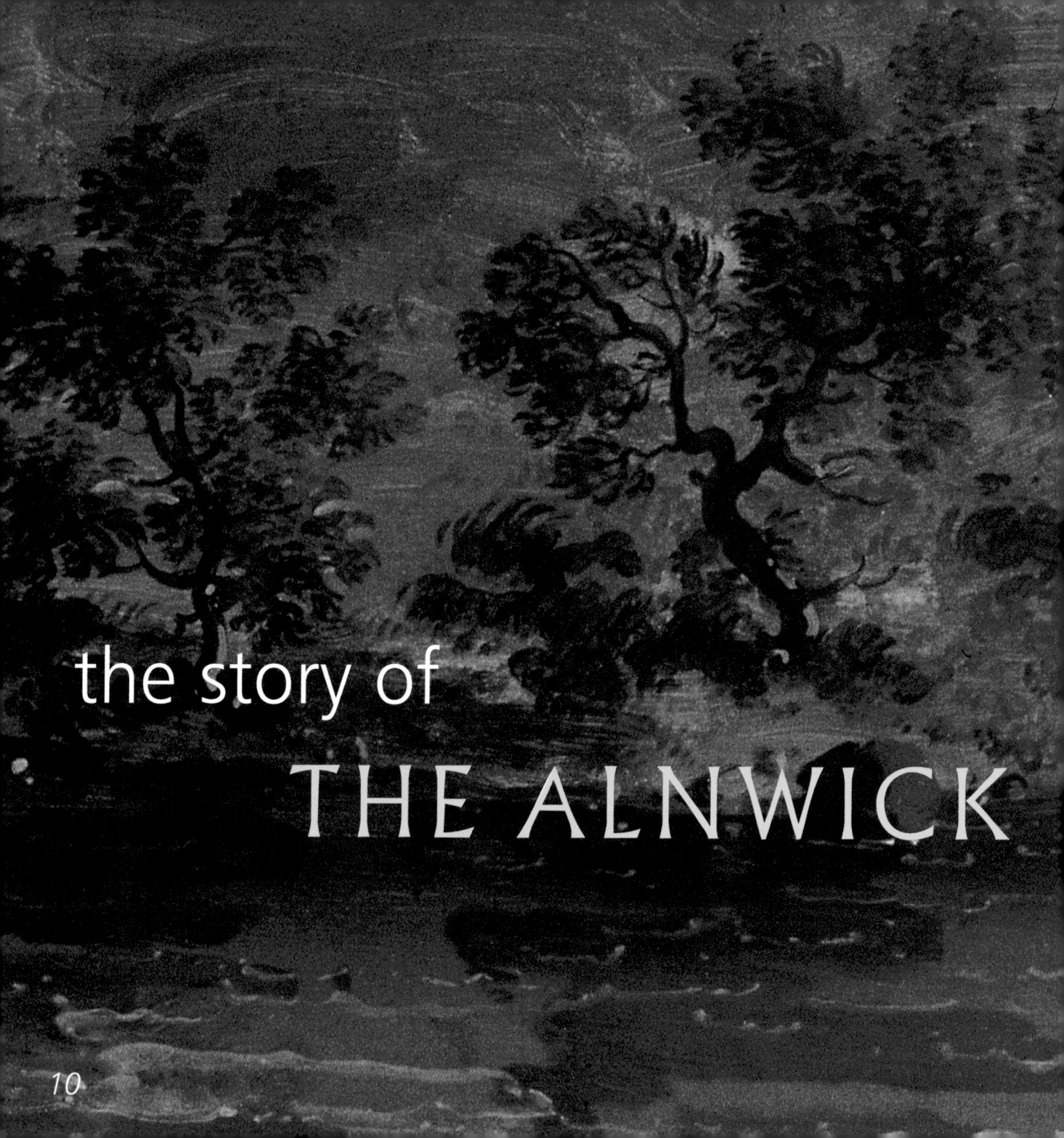

the story of THE ALNWICK

A detail from Canaletto's painting of Alnwick Castle in 1752

GARDEN is a remarkable one

Clockwise:
The Dukes of Northumberland - 1st, 2nd, 3rd, 4th

a brief history

From their humble beginnings in the mid-18th century the gardens had developed into one of Europe's finest by the end of the 19th century. Their founders, especially the first four dukes, enjoyed unrivalled reputations as men of science, patrons of botanists, collectors of exotic specimens and promoters of gardening excellence. Alnwick Castle Gardens in the North balanced the truly exceptional botanical magnificence of the dukes' conservatory gardens and grounds at Syon in the South. Proof of their early reputation rests in the visit to Alnwick of Czar Alexander I's head gardener in the 1800s and the spiriting away of the Alnwick head gardener to Russia. An early example of international 'head-hunting'. Of equal importance to the scale of investment and the skill of gardening technique was the inculcation in the Victorian era of the popular idea, formulated and implemented by the dukes, that the gardens should be popularly enjoyed by the general public. So the gardens became for a century a centre for popular interest and visits, made possible by the railway age.

After a final fling in the campaign of 'Digging for Victory' in the Second World War, the gardens took the full force of austere, post-war economic climate of retrenchment and were stripped to the level of barest maintenance.

a new era

Coming to the gardens in 1995 with a fresh mind and energy, the 12th Duchess visualised their one-time beauty and glory. She determined to create a classically designed garden, which contained water in every possible space, and the water had to come alive using the latest technology. The water was then to be enhanced with spectacular lighting. The Alnwick Garden will once more stand alongside the best gardens in Europe.

Visitors to The Garden will notice an interesting juxtaposition of old and new.

The Cascade, using the latest computer technology to control its fabulous water displays, is framed by two banks of earth laid out in 1850.

Four 16th century Venetian wrought iron gates, bought by the 4th Duke have been restored and replaced.

Two Northumbrian quarries were re-opened to provide stone for the outside walls of the Cascade and to match original stonework within The Garden.

a garden for the people

The Garden is contributing to the regeneration of a rural community as tourism takes on a new level of importance. As well as a unique meeting place for local people, The Garden provides an opportunity for people of all ages to learn new skills.

An education programme will develop a variety of courses throughout the year. People of any age will be able to join in the magic that is The Alnwick Garden. Put simply, a magnificent new public garden has been created in the North of England for the enjoyment of all.

vision to reality

View to the west, 1999, awaiting the archaeologists.

Opposite: Aerial view of The Garden from the north, showing development of the Cascade and Water Basin, the Ornamental Garden to the south, Rose Garden at the west side and to the east the car parks.

The Tower Crane operator's view of the Cascade and lower basin under construction.

The Ornamental Garden, May 2000.

Triple arch into original top walled Garden.

Remains of the last conservatory.

The 1850 pond - used by the Percy family as a skating rink in past winters.

ten steps to heaven

Below:
October 2000
The Ornamental Garden path construction - the first of two and a half miles within the Walled Garden.

Below:
November 2000
Water pipes supplying the water features in the Ornamental Garden.

Above:
April 2000
Archaeological survey revealed six separate levels of garden development since 1750.

Above:
October 2000
The Courtyard - formed with 88,000 Flemish paving bricks.

Above:
December 2000
Lower Basin reinforcement outlined in the snow. These areas will form the underground reservoirs to store 1,125,000 litres of water required to create the water displays.

Below:
February 2000
Pouring concrete during the construction of the source pool in the Ornamental Garden.

Above:
February 2000
The first pleached Red Sentinal crab apples arrive - secured on their bamboo frameworks.

Below:
March 2001
Circular pool and rill - Ornamental Garden.

Above:
August 2001
The Ornamental Garden.

Below:
August 2001
Red Sentinal crab apples - the first set.

Artist's impression of the Grand Cascade.

the Grand Cascade

The Garden's centrepiece is the Grand Cascade, a magnificent tumbling mass of water, ending in an eruption of fountains sending 350 litres of water six metres into the air every second.

Alternating sequences are controlled by state of the art technology.

A computer system synchronises the sensational displays and controls the 120 water jets within the Cascade.

850 twelve year old hornbeams (carpinus betulus) form the pergola framing the Grand Cascade.

31,500 litres per minute run down the Cascade at peak flow.

The trees surrounding the circular fountains are fastigiated oaks, variety 'Kosta'. The habit of this tree is that it grows perpendicular, or in a straight column, rather than spreading. The water fountain in the larger pool is set to a maximum height so as to be no higher than the top of the trees.

The Cascade's main feature comprises 120 water jets, 40 each side, plus 40 up the middle of the Cascade. The lower basin has a further 38 jets to create the volcano pushing up to 350 litres of water six metres into the air every second. The water used in every feature is filtered, purified, and recycled in vast pump rooms located under the Grand Cascade.

the Ornamental Garden

Opposite:
The Ornamental Garden has been created in a more formal style using symmetrical planting. Box hedge and yew are used to surround the various beds and borders. Laid end to end, there is over a mile of box hedge. Planting features unusual types and varieties of herbaceous perennials not usually seen in Britain, eg, 'Bevans' variety of geranium – please ask our Garden team for more details of all planting.

In the autumn splendid clusters of crab apples can be seen on pleached lines darkening to blood red and amber as the days shorten.

The dovecote is home to our family of Tumbler Doves, released into The Garden by The Duchess of Northumberland.

The Ornamental Garden has over 15,000 plants, shrubs and trees.

The entrance to the Ornamental Garden is through the magnificent archway. The stone is original and dates back to the late 18th century. The ornamental wrought iron gates are 16th century and have been painstakingly restored to their former glory.

Huge Delphiniums, some 3 metres high, adorn The Garden with two showings a year.

In the Rose Garden some 2,500 old highly scented shrubs roses mingle with other rose varieties to create a stunning summer display.

The first flush in the Rose Garden.

Breathtaking colour, old-world charm and rich fragrance are provided by cascades of old roses, which have wonderful scent and flower form. Some of the cultivars, centuries old, incude Officinalis the 'apothecary's rose' dating back prior to the 16th century, Rosa Mundi, Tuscany Superb and Louis Odier to name but a few.

the Rose Garden

Roses sponsored by David Austin include 50 of his "English Rose" cultivars.

Among over 180 varieties of roses within The Garden is the rose 'Alnwick Castle' launched at the Chelsea Flower Show in 2001.

The Fox sculpture stands at the end of the Rose Garden's winding path.

Clematis and Honeysuckle interwoven on a huge pergola add more scent, texture and colour.

Over 65,000 plants have been used in phase one of the garden.

The roses have kindly been donated by world famous rose grower David Austin, who has dedicated his life to breeding some of the most beautiful roses, the fragrant English Roses.

The Woodland Walk provides a contrast to the more formal gardens. Spring flowers and wild garlic carpet the ground along the walk.

the Woodland Walk

From the Walk, wonderful views of the Capability Brown landscape and Alnwick Castle can be enjoyed.

THE ALNWICK
GARDEN

throughout the year at The Alnwick Garden

January - Low winter sunlight emphasises the architectural beauty of The Garden. Crab apples, Malus Red Sentinel and Malus Evereste are brilliant against the hoar frost and snow.

February - Tens of thousands of spring bulbs emerge, first snowdrops then aconites.

March - Chinodoxas, Scillas and Daffodils adorn the approach to the Ornamental Garden from the Water Tower walk. The hedges show the lemon florets of the Cornus Mas before the foliage arrives.

April - Cherry is the first blossom in The Garden with apple following.

May - Early roses on the south wall of the Rose Garden. The herbaceous borders in the Ornamental Garden are a riot of colours, punctuated by the unusual Black Iris *germanica.*

June - Pergolas covered with Montana Clematis, Honeysuckle and climbing roses. The first Delphiniums bloom and the raspberry scent of the rose 'Alnwick Castle' fills the air.

July - Unusual soft fruits appear - Yellow Wonder strawberries, red and white raspberries. Cascades of highly perfumed old roses bloom, such as Rosa Mundi introduced to Britain in 1650.

August - The red rose of Lancaster, introduced to England in 1300, blooms. In the Ornamental Garden, the triangular Cornus Mas surround 'rooms' of unusual varieties of hydrangea. Subtle shades of hardy geraniums create ground cover throughout the borders.

September - Autumn fruits and the beginning of colour change in the Hornbeams create a new atmosphere around the Cascade.

October - Autumnal hues of rich orange, red and yellow on the blueberries, plum trees and climbers on the rose pergolas. The foliage of the unusual varieties of cherry tree change through dark red to purple hues.

November - Lupins and Delphiniums have their second flowering and the glistening red of the crab apples enlivens the bare branches of the trees.

December - Winter flowering Hellebores arrive. 'The Bride' cherry blossom flowers, and roses are still blooming. Look for one on your table in The Garden Café when you order your hot mince pies.

Friends of The Garden

We operate a Friends scheme which allows you unlimited access to enjoy this spectacular new public garden across the seasons.

Becoming a Friend of The Alnwick Garden entitles you to visit The Garden and use the Woodland Walk as many times as you wish for a one off annual payment - please pick up a leaflet for more information.

As a Friend, you will receive:

- A quarterly newsletter telling you all about the latest developments at The Garden and what to look out for on your next visit.
- Advance notice of events and activities
- Invitations to special days

To join, please obtain an application form from the admissions kiosk, the gift shop, or just call us. Complete the form, then either hand it to the admissions kiosk or send your form, along with your cheque (made payable to The Alnwick Garden) to:

Friends Administrator
The Alnwick Garden
Denwick Lane
Alnwick
Northumberland
NE66 1YU
Tel: 01665 511350
email: info@alnwickgarden.com

Your membership card and first newsletter will be sent to you within 28 days

Education, training & learning at The Alnwick Garden

The Alnwick Garden:

- seeks to provide a full educational programme to give people of all ages an opportunity to develop new skills and to promote lifelong learning;
- is a natural and cultural resource for the garden enthusiast, keen learner, school child and general interest visitor;
- is inspiring; educational and accessible to anyone regardless of age, physical abilities or location.
- will offer programmes in the arts and sciences covering national curriculum, lifelong learning, and leisure;
- seeks to establish a network with education and learning provision in the North East and beyond.

Initial Programme

- Botanical painting using garden specimens
- Beginners to master classes in botanical drawing and illustration
- School groups programme: science and technology based on water and the forces
- Story walks and creative story writing based on The Garden
- Ongoing development as a centre of excellence for the creative mind

- **Please phone 01665 511350 for details**